Raleigh
and the State of NORTH CAROLINA

It's big
but friendly too!

It's fun
with lots to do!

NORTH CAROLINA
Raleigh

The places where you live and visit help shape who you become. So find out all you can about the special places around you!

Cool Stuff™

A statue of Sir Walter Raleigh stands in front of the Progress Energy Center for the Performing Arts in Raleigh.

CREDITS

Series Concept and Development
Kate Boehm Jerome

Design
Steve Curtis Design, Inc. (www.SCDchicago.com); Roger Radtke, Todd Nossek

Reviewers and Contributors
Ryan Smith, Director of Communications, Greater Raleigh Convention and Visitors Bureau; Connie Bodner, Ph.D, senior researcher and writer; Judy Elgin Jensen, research and production; Mary L. Heaton, copy editor

Photography
Cover(a), Back Cover(a), i(a), xvi(f) © Konstantin L/Shutterstock; Cover(b), Back Cover(b), i(b) 7505811966/Shutterstock; Cover(c), Sights and Sounds (d) © Greg Snyder; Cover(d), xvi(a, h) © Zhong Chen/Shutterstock; ii, Strange But True (b), Marvelous Monikers (a) By Jmturner/from Wikimedia; iii, xvi(e) © ying/Shutterstock; Spotlight (background) © Filipe B. Varela/Shutterstock; Spotlight (a, b), By The Numbers (c), Sights and Sounds (e, g), Strange But True (a), Marvelous Monikers (c), xvi(c, d, g) Courtesy GRCVB/visitRaleigh.com; By The Numbers (a) © Matej Krajcovic/iStockphoto; By The Numbers (b) © peresanz/Shutterstock; By The Numbers (d) Yuri Arcurs/Shutterstock; Sights and Sounds (a) © Alenavlad/Shutterstock; Sights and Sounds (b) © Erin May; Sights and Sounds (c) © Michael C. Gray/Shutterstock; Sights and Sounds (f), xvi(b) © Bernd W. Herrmann/Shutterstock; Strange But True (c) © Rachel Strombeck/Visual Art Exchange/SPARKcon; Marvelous Monikers (b) © David T Brown; Marvelous Monikers (d) © Don Kennedy; Dramatic Days (a) © The Research Triangle Foundation of North Carolina; Dramatic Days (b) From NOAA; Dramatic Days (c) © JPerez/Shutterstock

Illustration
i © Jennifer Thermes/Photodisc/Getty Images

ISBN 978-1-4396-0096-2

Library of Congress Catalog Card Number: 2010935899

Published by Arcadia Publishing, Charleston, SC

For all general information contact Arcadia Publishing at:

Telephone 843-853-2070

Fax   843-853-0044

Email   sales@arcadiapublishing.com

For Customer Service and Orders:
Toll-Free   1-888-313-2665

Visit us on the Internet at www.arcadiapublishing.com

Table of Contents

Spotlight on Raleigh!

Raleigh is the capital of North Carolina. The city was named in honor of the sixteenth-century English explorer Sir Walter Raleigh.

Q: How many people call Raleigh home?

A: The population within city limits is around 400,000. But more than a million people live in the area that includes Raleigh and nearby Cary.

Q: Are there any sports teams in Raleigh?

A: Absolutely! Raleigh fans support such teams as the Carolina Hurricanes (hockey), the Carolina Mudcats (baseball), and the Carolina Railhawks (soccer). They also cheer for the college and university teams in the area!

Q: What's one thing every kid should know about Raleigh?

A: In order to get a central location for business, the state's General Assembly voted in 1792 to develop the site where Raleigh now stands—and bought 1,000 acres from Wake County resident Joel Lane to start the process.

Mister Wuf stirs up plenty of team spirit at North Carolina State University Wolfpack games.

Raleigh...

By The Numbers

1840

The North Carolina State Capitol was completed in 1840—almost a decade after a fire destroyed the first State House. The exterior walls of the current building are made of granite that was hauled to the site in horse-drawn cars of North Carolina's first railway.

700

According the Marbles Kids Museum, it would take about 700 marbles to fill up a child's head. The museum is a great place to "use your marbles" to discover new and interesting things—while you play!

79,464

The Cree Shimmer Wall on the Raleigh Convention Center is a moving work of art made of 79,464 light and dark aluminum squares that change shape and disappear as they flutter in the wind. At night the wall is backlit with special lights that can be programmed to flash—in more than a million different color combinations!

70

The farthest balcony seat in the Fletcher Opera Theatre is only 70 feet from the stage. It's part of the Progress Energy Center for the Performing Arts, which also includes such venues as the Meymandi Concert Hall, the Memorial Auditorium, the Kennedy Theater, and the two-acre Lichtin Plaza.

More Numbers!

1865	In that year, Shaw University was established in Raleigh.
1887	In that year, North Carolina State University was established in Raleigh.
37	At last count, the RBC Center offered 37 public restrooms.

Raleigh: Sights and Sounds

Hear

…beautiful music from not one, but two, symphony orchestras. Both the Raleigh Symphony and the North Carolina Symphony perform in the city.

Smell

…the fresh fruits and vegetables at the year round State Farmers Market in Raleigh.

…all the great food at the Raleigh Wide Open street festival. A walk up and down Fayetteville Street will surely fill you up!

See

...the Terror of the South exhibit at the North Carolina Museum of Natural Sciences. You can't miss the huge (and rare!) *Acrocanthosaurus* skeleton.

...the historic gristmill at Yates Mill County Park. (The gristmill uses water power to turn huge stones to grind wheat into flour and corn into cornmeal.)

Explore

...the North Carolina Museum of History to learn all about the state's rich past.

...the "outside art" that dots the landscape of Museum Park at the North Carolina Museum of Art.

STRANGE BUT TRUE!

ACORN AWEIGH!

Raleigh has a special tradition on New Year's Eve. Each year a crane hoists a giant 1,250-pound copper and steel acorn into the air, then "drops" it to mark the beginning of the New Year. Why an acorn? Check out the city's nickname when you get to the Marvelous Moniker pages. By the way, when the acorn sculpture is not in use on New Years Eve, you can see it on display in Moore Square.

A CAPTIVE CREW

The current governor's mansion in Raleigh (completed in 1891) had an interesting construction crew. In order to save money, inmates from the state prison helped build the Victorian-style building. Some prisoners molded bricks (out of Wake County clay) and signed their names or initials on them. If you look carefully at the bricks around the sidewalk of the mansion, you may be able to spot a few still marked by the men who made them.

STREET ART

SPARKcon is a huge celebration of creativity that is held in Raleigh each year. From fashion to photography, talent is showcased around the city in different "sparks," or themes. One of the highlights is the artSPARKS street painting event. Hundreds of artists chalk their creations onto Fayettville Street, turning it into a huge horizontal piece of art!

Strange But True

Raleigh: Marvelous Monikers

What's a moniker? It's another word for a name...and Raleigh has plenty of interesting monikers around town!

City Market

A Historic Name

The original **City Market** opened in 1914 to provide a place for farmers to sell produce, flowers, and other goods. Today City Market is known for its restaurants and stores—and it's still a good place for people to shop.

Raleigh Trolley

A Rhyming Name

The **Raleigh Trolley** is as much fun to say as it is to ride! On many Saturdays throughout the year, Historic Raleigh Trolley tours begin in Mordecai Historic Park where you can see the birthplace of the seventeenth president of the United States, Andrew Johnson.

Pullen Park

An Outdoor Treat

Enjoy the outdoors at **Pullen Park**. There's plenty to do—from baseball to pedal boats—and you can even ride the C.P. Huntington Train, a one-third sized replica (or copy) of a locomotive built in 1863.

NC State Fair

A Name for Fun

Raleigh is home to the **North Carolina State Fair**. With everything from prize-winning pumpkins to foot-stomping music, the fair is always a good time.

City of Oaks

A Natural Nickname

Since Raleigh has so many beautiful oak trees, it's often called the **City of Oaks**.

Marvelous Monikers

Raleigh:
DRAMATIC DAYS

A BIG
Idea!

THE RESEARCH TRIANGLE P
HEADQUARTERS

Big changes came to the Raleigh-Durham-Cary area in 1959 with the founding of the 7,000-acre Research Triangle Park. (The Triangle part of the name is a nod to the three major research universities in the area: North Carolina State University, Duke University, and the University of North Carolina-Chapel Hill.) From air pollution research to 3-D ultrasound technology, the scientists and researchers at the high-tech park have been involved in some really important scientific work—and who knows what exciting discoveries await?

A Hard Hit!

Hurricane Fran slammed into the east coast on September 5, 1996, and began its trek toward Raleigh. Because Fran was so large, the storm remained strong even as it traveled inland. Thus, hurricane force winds were felt in Raleigh and flooding was widespread. Fifty percent of the trees in the city were damaged.

Sadly, Fran's fury even cost some lives in North Carolina. Since it was so destructive, "Fran" has been retired from the list of future hurricane names.

A Heavy Snow!

Heavy snow began to fall on Raleigh around midnight on January 25, 2000. Before it was over, more than 20 inches of the white stuff had landed on the city. Unfortunately, most forecasters did not predict the big snowstorm, so many residents were caught off guard as power lines snapped and the snow piled into drifts. The good news about the Blizzard of 2000 is that forecasters now think they have a better way to predict such storms in future.

Congratulations!

You have just completed a kid-sized tour of Raleigh... but there's more to explore!

The city of Raleigh is an important part of the state of North Carolina. Why? It's because the city helps shape the state and the state helps shape the city!

Read on to find out more...

North Carolina

What's So Great About This State?

There is a lot to see and celebrate...just take a look!

CONTENTS

In North Carolina, you can drive from a beach on the Atlantic coast to the highest mountain peak east of the Mississippi River in less than a day.

Well, how about...
the land!

From the Beaches...

North Carolina is a beautiful state with more than 52,000 square miles of land. On the eastern side of the state, most of this land sits right at sea level. Why? It's because the Atlantic Ocean forms the eastern border of the state.

Millions of people enjoy the wonderful beaches along the barrier islands and sounds, or inlets. However, most of the state's population lives farther west in the middle part of the state. Here, gently rolling hills slowly begin to rise in elevation.

North Carolina beaches are beautiful summer vacation spots. Commercial and sport fishing are also big activities along the coast.

Tar from the pine trees that grow throughout North Carolina was an important part of the state's early economy and gave rise to the nickname the Tar Heel State (that really began to "stick" after the Civil War).

...To the Mountains

The huge 1,500-mile Appalachian Mountain range passes through the western part of North Carolina. This means that the Tar Heel State has many mountains—including the famous Blue Ridge and Great Smoky mountain chains. The highest mountain peak in the state, Mount Mitchell (elevation 6,684 feet), is also the highest peak east of the Mississippi!

North Carolina has amazingly beautiful land. So take a closer look at the next few pages to get a "big picture" view. Then decide which areas you might want to explore some more.

The Blue Ridge Parkway is a highway (with incredible engineering!) that winds through North Carolina's Blue Ridge Mountains.

The Cullasaja Falls are in the Nantahala National Forest, which is the largest of the four national forests in North Carolina.

The Oconaluftee River flows through Great Smoky Mountains National Park in North Carolina.

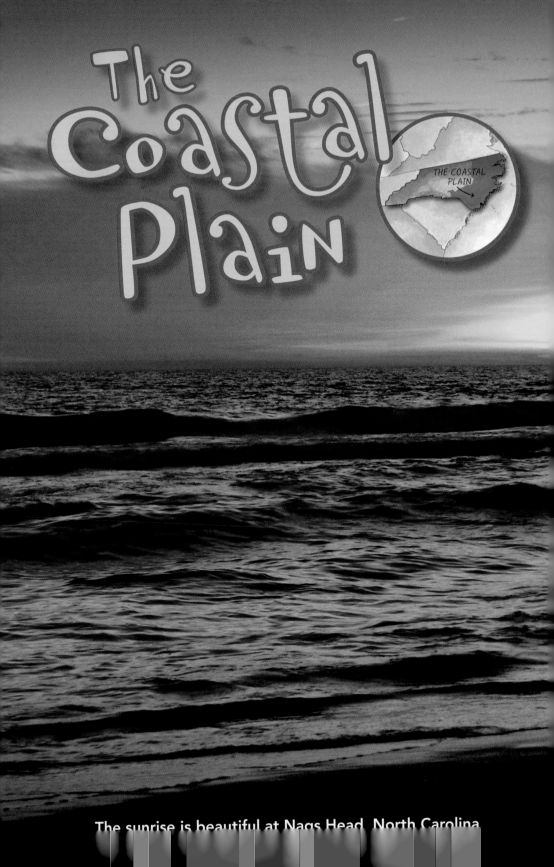

The Coastal Plain

THE COASTAL PLAIN

The sunrise is beautiful at Nags Head, North Carolina.

The Coastal Plain is the largest region in North Carolina. Three different areas—the Outer Banks, the Tidewater, and the Inner Coastal Plain—each contribute to the unique character of this region.

What's so special about the Outer Banks?

The Outer Banks protect much of the North Carolina coastline from the crashing waves of the open sea. Over one hundred miles of barrier islands form the easternmost part of the Outer Banks. Three areas that jut out from the mainland, called capes, are also part of the Outer Banks. Cape Hatteras, Cape Lookout, and Cape Fear are known for both their beauty and their dangerous underwater shifting sands.

So where is the Tidewater area?

The Tidewater starts just west of the Outer Banks. Much of this area is covered with wetlands. Many rivers and streams empty into the sounds, or inlets, of the Tidewater area. The Pamlico, Albemarle, Currituck, Croatan, Roanoke, Core, and Bogue Sounds are the seven sounds in the Tidewater.

The Tidewater also includes the Great Dismal Swamp. Its name doesn't sound very pleasant, but the swamp is home to a large variety of different kinds of mammals, reptiles, amphibians, and birds—not to mention insects and plants, of course.

...and there's more!

Just west of the Tidewater is the higher, drier land of the Inner Coastal Plain. Its rich, sandy soil forms some of the best farmland in the state.

The famous Cape Hatteras Lighthouse shines a light that can be seen twenty miles out at sea.

Carnivorous, or meat-eating, Venus Flytrap plants grow naturally in the North Carolina Tidewater.

5

The Piedmont

THE PIEDMONT

Lake Norman is a large inland lake in the Piedmont region that has 520 miles of shoreline.

The Piedmont region lies in the middle of North Carolina. Piedmont means "foot of the mountain," and its land gently rises from about 300 feet on its eastern boundary to around 1,500 feet along its western boundary, which is closest to the mountains.

What's so special about the Piedmont region?

The rolling hills of the Piedmont are famous for their historic towns and golf courses. But there are also tobacco, cotton, and soybean farms as well as acres of vineyards in the region. The clay soil from some areas is used to make pottery. Minerals, including gold and emeralds, have also been found in this region.

Spotted salamanders live in many parts of the state—including the Piedmont region.

What can I see in the Piedmont?

Well, one thing you can see is people! More North Carolinians live in this region than anywhere else in the state. Big cities such as Charlotte, Durham, Greensboro, and the state's capital, Raleigh, are found here. Many of the state's big universities are also in the Piedmont area.

Don't forget about the fall line!

The Piedmont region is separated from the Coastal Plain region by an imaginary fall line. The land to the west of the fall line is higher than the land to the east. As a result, waterfalls can occur in Piedmont rivers and streams as they "fall" onto the lower land of the Coastal Plain.

Charlotte, the largest city in North Carolina, is in the Piedmont region of the state.

The Mountains

THE MOUNTAINS

Mount Mitchell State Park has an icy look in the winter.

The Mountain region of North Carolina is the smallest region in the state in terms of area—but not in height! More than one hundred of its mountains rise to 5,000 feet, and more than forty mountains top 6,000 feet!

What's so special about the Mountain region?

Spectacular forests, amazing waterfalls, incredible peaks and cliffs—it's hard to describe the natural beauty of this region! Even the names of some of the mountain ranges are attempts to describe their unique look. The very dark evergreen forests along their peaks give the Black Mountains their name. The Blue Ridge Mountains appear to have a hazy blue look from a distance. And the higher elevations of the Smoky Mountains are often shrouded in fog, which makes them look as if they're surrounded by smoke.

Don't forget about the gorges! (...and what exactly is a gorge, anyway?)

A gorge is a deep and narrow channel with steep rocky sides that are carved out over a long period of time—often by the rushing water of a river. The Linville Gorge in the Pigsah National Forest and the Nantahala Gorge in the Nantahala National Forest are two big gorges in North Carolina. Many valleys, such as the beautiful Maggie Valley, are also sprinkled throughout the region.

Grandfather Mountain's Mile-High Swinging Bridge is a mile above sea level—and swings over an 80-foot chasm, or drop.

At Chimney Rock State Park, a 26-story elevator (built right inside the mountain!) takes visitors to the top of Chimney Rock for great views of Lake Lure and Hickory Nut Gorge.

Well, how about...
the history!

Tell Me a Story!

The story of North Carolina begins thousands of years ago. Following the tradition of their ancestors who first lived on the land, Native Americans made their home throughout the state. Most lived in groups called tribes, and each had its own culture.

Native Americans living in North Carolina in the 1500s included such groups as the Catawbas, Tuscaroras, and Algonquins. However, the mountain-dwelling Cherokees had the largest communities.

The Museum of the Cherokee Indian in Cherokee, North Carolina, tells a 10,000-year history of this amazing Native American culture. Tragically, in 1838 most of the Cherokee were forced out of North Carolina. Their thousand-mile journey to Oklahoma—now remembered as the "Trail of Tears"—cost many lives. However, the Cherokee Nation managed to survive and descendants still live in North Carolina today.

Constructed more than one hundred years ago, the Biltmore Estate in Asheville is still the largest privately owned home in the United States.

...The Story Continues

Eventually, Spanish, French, and English explorers came to North Carolina as well as other European and American settlers and African Americans. Through the years many battles for freedom were fought in North Carolina—from the French and Indian War to the American Civil War.

But history isn't always about war. North Carolinians have always educated, invented, painted, written, sung, and built. Many footprints are stamped into the soul of North Carolina's history. You can see evidence of this all over the state!

North Carolina's Halifax Resolves (April 12, 1776) were the first official act by any of the 13 colonies to call for independence from British rule.

In the early 1900s, Dr. Charlotte Hawkins Brown was the founder and leader of the Palmer Memorial Institute, a school for African American students.

Monuments

Autumn leaves fall on this statue in Union Square in Raleigh which honors the three presidents who were born in North Carolina—James Polk, Andrew Jackson, and Andrew Johnson.

1795   1849
JAMES KNOX POLK
OF
MECKLENBURG COUNTY
PRESIDENT
1845 — 1849
HE ENLARGED OUR

1767   1845
ANDREW JACKSON
OF
UNION COUNTY
PRESIDENT
1829 — 1837
HE REVITALIZED

1808   18
ANDREW JOHNSON
OF
WAKE COUNTY
PRESIDENT
1865 — 1869
HE DEFENDED

Monuments and historic sites honor the special people and events that helped shape the state of North Carolina—and the nation.

What kind of monuments can I see in North Carolina?

There are many different kinds. From statues to bridges to street signs and fountains, almost every town has found some way to honor a historic person or event.

Where are monuments placed?

Almost anywhere! A plaque on top of Mt. Mitchell honors its namesake—the Reverend Elisha Mitchell.

What about historic sites?

North Carolina has plenty! For example, the Carl Sandburg Home is a historic site located on 264 acres in western North Carolina. It was the first historic site to honor an American poet.

The Duke Homestead in Durham is another historic site. It allows visitors to see the early farm and factory where Washington Duke first grew and processed tobacco.

The Freedmen's Colony Monument on Roanoke Island pays tribute to African Americans who escaped from slavery to begin a new life during the Civil War.

The Wright Brothers National Memorial in Kill Devil Hills honors the brothers' first successful airplane flights in 1903. Interestingly, Orville and Wilbur had a business selling, repairing, and manufacturing bicycles to pay for their flying experiments.

Museums

The North Carolina Transportation Museum in Spencer preserves the history of transportation in the state.

Museums don't just tell you about history—they actually show you artifacts from times past. (By the way, an artifact is any object that is actually produced by a human!)

Why are the museums throughout North Carolina so special?

North Carolina's museums contain amazing exhibits that tell the story of the state. For example, the North Carolina Museum of History in Raleigh has more than 250,000 historical items that piece together the state's history.

What can I see in a museum?

An easier question to answer might be "What can't I see in a museum?" Are you interested in fossils? The Aurora Fossil Museum has hundreds of whale and shark fossils. Visitors can even make their own discoveries by digging through the museum's special fossil pit.

The Franklin Gem & Mineral Museum displays another type of collection. It has beautiful precious and semiprecious stones—as well as a nice collection of Native American artifacts.

...and don't forget the kilts!

The Scottish Tartans Museum in Franklin tells the story of Scottish Highland clothing. This museum is located in North Carolina because the state is home to so many people of Scottish descent.

The *USS North Carolina* battleship rests as a floating museum at the port of Wilmington. This ship was a city at sea for two thousand sailors during World War II. Besides living, eating, and medical facilities, the ship even had such things as a movie theater and an ice cream shop.

How many buttons do you have? The Belhaven Memorial Museum builds on the unique collections of Mary Eva Blount Way. Before she died, "Miss Eva" collected approximately thirty thousand buttons from all over the world!

Plantations

The Hope Mansion was built in 1803.

In the early 1800s, the Hope Plantation near Windsor, North Carolina had its own water powered grist mill, a blacksmith shop, and a cooper's shop. (Coopers made containers, such as barrels and buckets.)

Why are plantations special?
(...and what is a plantation, anyway?)

Plantations were large estates or farms where crops such as rice and cotton were grown. Enslaved Africans did most of the work on a plantation.

Today, many plantations tell the shared history of our country. All have fascinating stories of race, culture, families, and sacrifice.

What can I see if I visit a plantation?

Some plantations show you what life was like hundreds of years ago. As you might guess, kitchens were very different in the 1800s. Meals were cooked on an open hearth with heavy cast iron cookware. And, there was no running water or refrigeration, either!

...and there's more!

Other plantations today grow beautiful gardens or help preserve nature in other ways. The Latta Plantation in Mecklenburg County is now a nature center and preserve. This former cotton plantation is now part of an effort to protect more than 1,343 acres of natural habitats.

Preparing meals on a plantation was a lot of work.

The American Bald Eagle, like this one, is one of the many species of birds whose habitats are protected at the Latta Plantation Nature Preserve.

Well, how about... the people!

Enjoying the Outdoors

More than nine million people live in the state of North Carolina. With so many people, you can be sure that there are lots of different opinions throughout the state. However, North Carolinians also have plenty in common.

Many share a love of the outdoors. The state has a mild climate, but it still has four seasons for people to enjoy. Surfing and swimming are popular at the Outer Banks in the summer, while skiing and snowboarding are favorite pastimes in the mountains in the winter. Hiking, fishing, golfing—the list of things that North Carolinians enjoy goes on and on!

Rock climbing is a popular activity at Chimney Rock State Park.

Golfers love the many great courses in North Carolina.

Sharing Traditions

The state of North Carolina is rich in traditions. Crafts like quilting and basket weaving are passed down through the generations. Even storytelling is an art in many places throughout the state.

Did you ever wonder what a Revolutionary War battle was like? North Carolinians sometimes re-create battles to honor the history and heritage of brave soldiers. Cooking is another way to pass on traditions. Have you ever heard of Moravian Sugar Cake? How about Calabash-style seafood? North Carolina kitchens are full of cherished recipes!

Pottery making in the Catawba Valley has been a traditional craft since colonial times.

Reenactors at Tryon Palace demonstrate what life was like in the late 1700s, when New Bern was the first permanent capital of the colony of North Carolina.

North Carolinians appreciate the beauty of the land around them.

Protecting

Without conservation efforts, the river otter might have disappeared from North Carolina. You can learn about them at the North Carolina Aquarium—which has three locations in the state.

The Karen Beasley Sea Turtle Rescue and Rehabilitation Center is in Topsail. Its mission is to conserve and protect sea turtles like the loggerhead shown here.

Protecting all of North Carolina's natural resources is a full-time job for many people!

Why is it important to protect North Carolina's natural resources?

The many different environments in North Carolina help shape its character. Life along the coast moves in rhythm with the tides and the water. Activities in the mountains are often dictated by altitudes and seasons. All these different environments also mean that many different plants and animals can live throughout the state. In technical terms, North Carolina has great biodiversity! This biodiversity is important to protect because it keeps the environments balanced and healthy.

What kinds of organizations protect these resources?

It takes a lot of groups to cover it all. The U.S. Fish and Wildlife Service is a national organization. The state's main environmental agency is the Department of Environment and Natural Resources. The state's park system is part of this agency.

Education programs at the North Carolina Zoo in Asheboro teach visitors about different animals and their habitats.

And don't forget...

You can make a difference, too! It's called "environmental stewardship"—and it means you are willing to take personal responsibility to help protect North Carolina's natural resources.

Creating Jobs

A gigantic chest of drawers in High Point—furniture manufacturing has been important in the state for a long time.

North Carolina grows more sweet potatoes than any other state.

Some jobs, such as farming, furniture making, and textile production have been done in North Carolina for a long time. Other jobs, such as filmmaking, medical research, and banking, are growing in demand.

Why is North Carolina a good place to work?

The state has great natural resources and energetic people! These two things help businesses grow.

What kinds of jobs are available throughout the state?

North Carolinians have always been good at making things. Today, many people work in the manufacturing industry. From furniture and fabrics to paper products, electrical machinery, computers, and chemicals, great products come through warehouses all over the state.

North Carolina is home to great medical and research facilities.

The state also has mineral resources and leads the nation in the production of materials made from feldspar, mica, and lithium.

Another big industry is the service industry. From chefs to tour guides, many jobs are needed to help tourists sightsee, eat, and relax!

Don't forget the military!

The Air Force, Army, Marine Corps, Navy, and Coast Guard can all be found in the state. North Carolinians have great respect for all the brave men and women who serve our country.

Military training is hard work!

celebrating

Lots of People have fun at the North Carolina
Mountain State Fair.

The people of North Carolina really know how to have fun! Not only do they celebrate the State Fair in Raleigh each year—they also have a Mountain State Fair in Fletcher as well.

Why are North Carolina festivals and celebrations special?

Celebrations and festivals bring people together. From cooking contests to art shows, events in every corner of the state showcase all different kinds of people and talents.

What kind of celebrations and festivals are held in North Carolina?

Too many to count! But one thing is for sure. You can find a celebration for just about anything you want to do.

Would you like a pickle? The Mount Olive Pickle Festival will provide you with free pickles and the opportunity to shake hands with the eight-foot pickle himself, Mr. Crisp.

How about a weather forecast from a woolly worm? Since 1978, the people of Banner Elk have been racing their worms at the Woolly Worm Festival. The winning worm has the honor of predicting the weather for the coming winter.

...and don't forget about the Hollerin' contest!

In earlier times, neighbors in the country often communicated by loudly calling across the fields. You might think it was yelling; but it was hollerin'. That tradition may have disappeared, but it is celebrated each year at the National Hollerin' Contest in Spiveys Corner.

Artistic statues of pigs are placed around the city of Lexington each year in a public art project called "Pigs in the City." The pig art sets the stage for Lexington's famous Barbecue Festival that takes place every fall.

You can enjoy grilled shrimp—and plenty of other seafood—at the North Carolina Seafood Festival in Morehead City.

Birds and Words

What do all the people of North Carolina have in common? These symbols represent the state's shared history and natural resources.

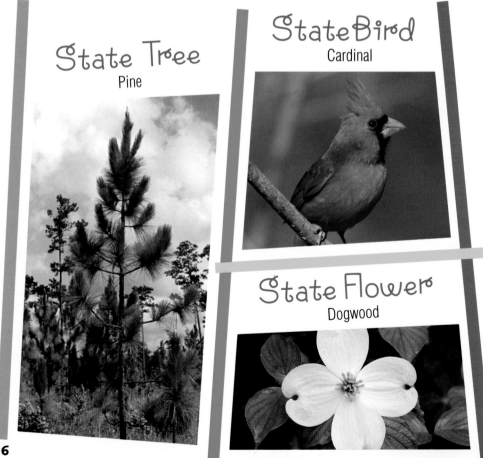

State Tree
Pine

State Bird
Cardinal

State Flower
Dogwood

State Berries
Strawberry and Blueberry

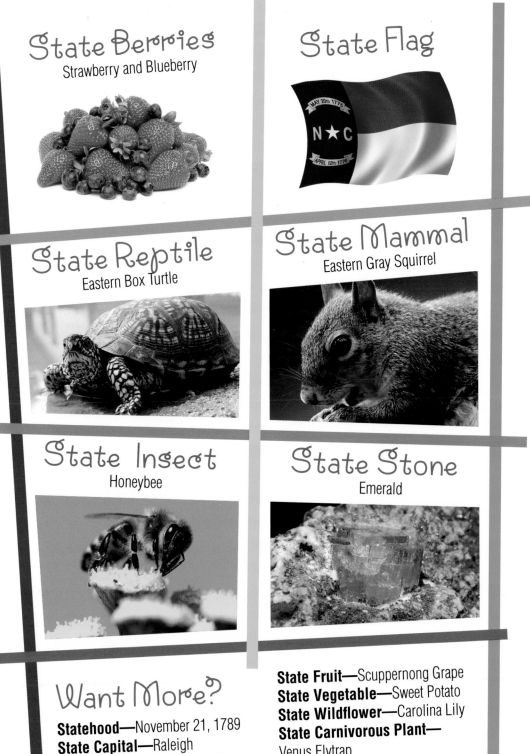

State Flag

State Reptile
Eastern Box Turtle

State Mammal
Eastern Gray Squirrel

State Insect
Honeybee

State Stone
Emerald

Want More?

Statehood—November 21, 1789
State Capital—Raleigh
State Nickname—Tar Heel State
State Song—"The Old North State"
State Rock—Granite
State Beverage—Milk

State Fruit—Scuppernong Grape
State Vegetable—Sweet Potato
State Wildflower—Carolina Lily
State Carnivorous Plant—
Venus Flytrap
State Shell—Scotch Bonnet
State Motto—"*Esse Quam Videri*"
("To be rather than to seem")

More Fun Facts

More

Here's some more interesting stuff about North Carolina.

The Northern Half

In 1629, King Charles I of England directedthat all the land from Albermarle Sound to the St. Johns River be called Carolana. His son, Charles II, changed the name to Carolina. When Carolina was eventually divided, the northern part became North Carolina.

The Lost Colony

A group of English colonists led by John White settled on Roanoke Island in 1587. When supplies ran short, White sailed back to England. However, when he returned to Roanoke in 1590, he found just a few remains of the colony. To this day no one is completely sure what happened to the colony and its settlers.

A Pirate's Cove

The notorious pirate, Blackbeard, stayed for a time in **Bath**—North Carolina's first established town.

First in Its Class

The first state university in the United States—the University of North Carolina—opened in 1795 in **Chapel Hill**.

Lights, Camera, Action

Some movies made in North Carolina include *Blue Velvet*, *The Color Purple*, *The Hunt for Red October*, *Days of Thunder*, and *Patch Adams*.

Fore!

The first miniature golf course in the United States was built in **Pinehurst** in 1916.

Right in the Center

The geographic center of North Carolina is in Chatham County, 10 miles northwest of **Sanford**.

Universities Unite

Three major research universities—Duke University in **Durham**, North Carolina State University in **Raleigh**, and the University of North Carolina in **Chapel Hill**—are part of North Carolina's Research Triangle Park.

Green with Envy

The largest emerald crystal ever found in North America came from the Piedmont area in North Carolina.

Brad's Drink

A cola invented in 1893 by Caleb Bradham of **New Bern** was first called "Brad's Drink." It later became known as Pepsi-Cola!

Bright Light

The **Cape Hatteras** Lighthouse is the tallest brick lighthouse in the United States.

Glazed Over

Krispy Kreme Doughnuts, Inc., was founded in **Winston-Salem**.

Coming Through!

The **Outer Banks** are part of the "Atlantic flyway," where thousands of birds can be spotted during their annual southward migration.

Bagpipe Brigade

Each year, Scottish clans get together in **Linville** at the Grandfather Mountain Highland Games. Competitions include the hammer throw and the clan tug-of-war!

Helping Madagascar

The Duke Lemur Center is the world's largest sanctuary for rare and endangered prosimian primates—including ring-tailed lemurs!

Shooting Par

Pinehurst is known for its beautiful golf courses. But between 1916 and 1920, Annie Oakley (the sharp-shooting star of Buffalo Bill's Wild West Show) was in charge of the Pinehurst Gun Club where she gave shooting exhibitions and lessons.

Born to Race

North Carolina has deep roots with NASCAR. The state is the birthplace and home of many NASCAR legends including Dale Earnhardt (both Senior and Junior) and Richard Petty.

Wild Rivers

North Carolina has some popular whitewater rafting rivers including the Nantahala and the French Broad rivers.

Find Out More

There are many great websites that can give you more information about the exciting things that are going on in the state of North Carolina!

State Websites

The Official Government Website of North Carolina
www.ncgov.com

North Carolina Highway Historical Marker Program
www.ncmarkers.com

North Carolina State Parks
www.ncparks.gov

The Official Travel and Tourism Site of North Carolina
www.visitnc.com

Museums/Asheboro

North Carolina Aviation Museum
www.ncairmuseum.org

Asheville

Ashville Art Museum
www.ashevilleart.org

Charlotte

North Carolina Mint Museum
www.mintmuseum.org

Cherokee

Museum of the Cherokee Indian
www.cherokeemuseum.org

Greensboro

International Civil Rights Center & Museum
www.sitinmovement.org

New Bern

Tryon Palace
www.tryonpalace.org

Raleigh

North Carolina Museum of Art
www.ncartmuseum.org

North Carolina Museum of History
www.ncmuseumofhistory.org

North Carolina Museum of Natural Sciences
www.naturalsciences.org

Wilmington

Battleship North Carolina
www.battleshipnc.com

Winston-Salem

SciWorks
www.sciworks.org

Aquariums and Zoos

North Carolina Aquariums
www.ncaquariums.com

North Carolina Zoo (Asheboro)
www.nczoo.org

Duke University Lemur Center (Durham)
www.lemur.duke.edu

North Carolina: At A Glance

State Capital: Raleigh

North Carolina Borders: South Carolina, Georgia, Tennessee, Virginia, and the Atlantic Ocean

Population: Over 9 million

Highest Point: Mount Mitchell at 6,684 feet above sea level

Lowest Point: Sea level at the Atlantic Ocean

Some Major Cities: Raleigh, Charlotte, Greensboro, Durham, Winston-Salem, Fayetteville, Cary, Wilmington, High Point, Asheville

Some Famous Tar Heels

Andy Griffith (born 1926) from Mount Airy; is an actor famous for his work on the long-running television series *The Andy Griffith Show* and *Matlock*.

Andrew Jackson (1767–1845) from the Waxhaw region; was the 7th President of the United States.

Junaluska (around 1775-1858) from Murphy area; was a Cherokee leader in western North Carolina.

Virginia Dare (1587–?) Roanoke Colony; was the first child born in the Americas to English parents.

Mary Elizabeth Dole (born 1936) from Salisbury, NC; is an American politician who became the first woman United States senator from North Carolina.

(Ralph) Dale Earnhardt Sr. (1951–2001) from Kannapolis, NC; was an American race car and NASCAR Hall of Famer.

Roberta Flack (born 1937) from Black Mountain, NC; is a Grammy-winning jazz and R & B singer.

Dolley Madison (1768–1849) from Guilford County; was First Lady of the United States (1809-1817) as the wife of the 4th President of the United States, James Madison.

James K. Polk (1795–1849) from Mecklenburg County; was the 11th President of the United States.

Charles Kuralt (1934–1997) from Wilmington; was an Emmy- and Peabody-award-winning journalist and television host.

Hiram Rhoades Revels (1822–1901) from Fayetteville; was the first African American member of the United States Congress.

The Cape Hatteras Lighthouse is a National Historic Landmark.

CREDITS

Series Concept and Development
Kate Boehm Jerome

Design
Steve Curtis Design, Inc. (www.SCDchicago.com); Roger Radtke, Todd Nossek

Reviewers and Contributors
Content review: Michael Hill and Ansley Wagner, North Carolina Office of Archives and History; Contributing writers/ediotrs: Terry B. Flohr; Stacey L.Klaman; Research and production: Judy Elgin Jensen; Copy Editor: Mary L. Heaton

Photography
Back Cover(a), Cover(d), 9b © Kenneth Wiedemann/iStockphoto; Back Cover(b), 10-11 Used with permission from The Biltmore Company, Asheville, North Carolina; Back Cover(c), 13b © David Ross/Shutterstock; Back Cover(d), Cover(a), 3b © Dave Allen Photography/Shutterstock; Back Cover(e) © Patrick Johnson/Shutterstock; Cover(b), 26(c) © Jonathan Larsen/Shutterstock; Cover(c), 2a © iofoto/Shutterstock; Cover(e) © Robert Ranson/Shutterstock; Cover(f) © Matej Krajcovic/iStockphoto; 2-3 © Eric Foltz/iStockphoto; 2a © Eldin/Shutterstock; 3a © Tim Mainiero/Shutterstock; 4-5 © jadimages/Shutterstock; 5a © Jorge Moro/Shutterstock; 5b © David Huntley/Shutterstock; 6-7 Courtesy Visit Lake Norman; 7a © Ryan M. Bolton/Shutterstock; 7b © Nick Martucci/Shutterstock; 8-9 By Matt Mutel, Courtesy NC Division of Parks and Recreation; 9a Ken Thomas/Wikimedia; 10a © Courtesy of the Eastern Band of Cherokee Indians; 11a © Lawrence Roberg/Shutterstock; 11b Courtesy Charlotte Hawkins Brown Museum, State Historic Sites, NC Dept. of Cultural Resources; 12-13 © Kevin Borland; 13a © Don Kennedy; 14-15 Courtesy North Carolina Transportation Museum; 15a © Paul MacKenzie/iStockphoto; 15b © Cre8tive Images/Shutterstock; 16-17 by James Veverka, Courtesy Hope Plantation; 17a By Jean Davis Olecki; 17b © Don Fink/Shutterstock; 18-19 © Bonita R. Cheshier/Shutterstock; 18a Courtesy Chimney Rock at Chimney Rock State Park; 18b © Jerry Zitterman/Shutterstock; 19a © Mikhail Olykainen/Shutterstock; 19b (Interactive historical interpreter) Courtesy Tryon Palace, North Carolina; 20-21 © Štěpán Ježek/iStockphoto; 21a © Mihai Dancaescu/Shutterstock; 21b N.C. Zoo photo; 22-23 By Brady Stern; 23a © CREATISTA/Shutterstock; 23b © l i g h t p o e t/Shutterstock; 23c © John Wollworth/Shutterstock; 24-25 By Susan Lee (leewaydesign.com); 25a By Dwayne Padon; 25b © Korolevskaya Nataliya/Shutterstock; 26a USDA Forest Service; 26b © Doug Lemke/Shutterstock; 27a © Kim Reinick/Shutterstock; 27b © Pakmor/Shutterstock; 27c © Constance McGuire/iStockphoto; 27d © Redwood/Shutterstock; 27e © Daniel Prudek/Shutterstock; 27f © Terry Davis/Shutterstock; 28a © artcalin/Shutterstock; 28b © Dewitt/Shutterstock; 29 © Karen Hadley/Shutterstock; 31 © R. Gino Santa Maria/Shutterstock; 32 © Jorge Moro/Shutterstock

Illustration
Back Cover, 1, 4, 6 © Jenníer Thermes/Photodisc/Getty Images

ISBN 978-1-58973-017-5

Library of Congress Catalog Card Number: 2010935881

1 2 3 4 5 6 WPC 15 14 13 12 11 10

Published by Arcadia Publishing, Charleston, SC

For all general information contact Arcadia Publishing at:

Telephone   843-853-2070

Fax   843-853-0044

Email   sales@arcadiapublishing.com

For Customer Service and Orders:

Toll Free   1-888-313-2665

Visit us on the Internet at www.arcadiapublishing.com